FUNGI POWER

FUNGI as RECYCLERS

Cherry Lake Press
Ann Arbor, Michigan

by Joyce Markovics

CHERRY LAKE PRESS

Published in the United States of America by
Cherry Lake Publishing Group
Ann Arbor, Michigan
www.cherrylakepublishing.com

Reading Adviser: Beth Walker Gambro, MS, Ed., Reading Consultant, Yorkville, IL

Content Adviser: David S. Hibbett, PhD, Clark University, Worcester, Massachusetts

Book Designer: Ed Morgan
Book Developer: Bowerbird Books

Photo Credits: © Ed Morgan, cover, title page, and table of contents; © davidclode/Unsplash.com, 4–5; © Vik Nanda/flickr.com, 6; © Doug Beckers/flickr.com, 7; © freepik.com, 8; © Ryan Hodnett/flickr.com, 9; © freepik.com, 10; © Alison Harrington/flickr.com, 11; © godi photo/Shutterstock, 12–13; © Katja Schulz/flickr.com, 14; © Syarifuddin Kate/Shutterstock, 15; Wilhelm Zimmerling PAR/Wikimedia Commons, 16; Daryl Thompson/Wikimedia Commons, 17; Keisotyo/Wikimedia Commons, 18; © freepik.com, 19, 20–21, 22; ESA, CC BY-SA IGO 3.0/Wikimedia Commons, 23; Medmyco/Wikimedia Commons, 24; NASA/Roscosmos, 25; ©freepik.com, 26–27; Vielfalt/Wikimedia Commons, 28; © freepik.com, 29 top, 29 bottom.

Cherry Lake Press is an imprint of Cherry Lake Publishing Group.

Library of Congress Cataloging-in-Publication Data has been filed and is available at catalog.loc.gov

Printed in the United States of America

CONTENTS

That Stinks!

Something stinks. It's hard to identify the **pungent** odor. It smells like a mix of rotten meat and a porta-potty. Or a garbage truck on a hot day. The disgusting smell attracts flies—lots of them. After buzzing around, the insects make their descent. They land on an orange-red growth with a cage-like top covered in slime. The smelly thing looks more like a pickleball than what it is. This strange **organism** is neither an animal nor a plant. It is a fungus (plural fungi)! More specifically, it's a lattice stinkhorn mushroom.

Stinkhorns grow in many shapes, sizes, and colors. They can be found in parks and gardens after rainstorms. Most resemble balls or horns. However, some look like the arms of an octopus. Others have lacy skirts.

Young lattice stinkhorn mushrooms could be mistaken for dirty chicken eggs. They appear in the soil. Then, in just minutes, the eggs balloon open. Smelly, slime-covered mushrooms pop up like magic.

The lattice stinkhorn mushroom is also called the devil's lantern or the witch's heart.

It's the slime, or gleba, that gives off the funky smell. The stinkhorn's stench may repel people. But flies love it. They slurp it up with their mouthparts. In the process, the mushroom's spores stick to the flies. Spores are tiny **cells** produced by fungi that grow into new fungi. The flies then spread the spores far and wide, aiding the stinkhorn in its **reproduction**. About 24 hours after they appear, lattice stinkhorn mushrooms shrivel up and disappear.

Flies on a stinkhorn fungus

This star-shaped stinkhorn feeds on wood chips.

What's even cooler about stinkhorns is their job. Stinkhorns help break down dead wood. They, along with many other kinds of fungi, are nature's recyclers. Fungi are "the garbage disposal agents of the natural world," according to **mycologist** Lynne Boddy. "They break down dead, **organic** matter, and by doing that, they release **nutrients**," said Lynne. "And those nutrients are then made available for plants to carry on growing."

FUNGI Facts

Stinkhorns can grow up to 6 inches (15 centimeters) per hour! And they're so powerful, they can break through pavement.

What Are Fungi?

You might not know it, but fungi are everywhere. They're in the soil and living on plants. Fungi are also on and in the bodies of animals, including humans! But what are fungi? And where did they come from? If they're neither animals nor plants, what are they? As it turns out, fungi are an entire group of **species**. Other fungi include yeasts, molds, and mildews. They range in size from teeny-tiny to enormous. Some experts think there are millions of kinds of fungi. However, only about 160,000 have been identified so far.

Mold, a type of fungus, grows on an orange.

Fungi likely **evolved** around 1 billion years ago. Close to 500 million years ago, plants began to grow on land. However, they didn't have well-developed roots. So, plants and fungi teamed up! Fungi helped plants get the nutrients they needed to survive. And plants shared their food with fungi. After tens of millions of years, plants developed roots. But plants and fungi still rely on each other for survival.

Liverworts (shown above) were some of the first plants to grow on Earth.

FUNGI Facts

The largest fungus in the world weighs hundreds of tons. It sprawls over an area that's as big as 180 football fields!

Plants create food through **photosynthesis**. They absorb sunlight. Then they use the Sun's energy to change water and **carbon dioxide** into sugar. Unlike plants, fungi can't make their own food. So, like animals, fungi must find food to eat.

Fungi start out as spores. The spores are often carried by the wind or by animals. When a spore lands on the ground or another suitable place, it **germinates**. Then it develops hyphae (HAHY-fey). These long threads are similar to the roots of a plant. Each one is thinner than a human hair. They form big bundles called mycelium (mahy-SEE-lee-uhm). The mycelium grows and expands. Have you ever seen a white, weblike material in a pile of rotting wood? That's mycelium.

Mycelium

FUNGI Facts

Mycelium grows one cell at a time! It can often extend for hundreds—or thousands—of miles if its hyphae were stretched end to end.

The mycelium's outer hyphae explore the soil to find food. When they locate food, they release chemicals called **enzymes**. The enzymes break down the food into smaller parts. Fungi not only feed themselves, but they also help plants. Sometimes, plants can't absorb water and nutrients. That's when fungi come in. They interconnect with plant roots. And they share water and nutrients with plants. In exchange, plants give fungi the sugars that they make through photosynthesis.

When fungi get the food and water they need, some species make mushrooms. Think of mushrooms as the fruiting part of fungi. They're only a small part of a much bigger organism. Mushrooms have an important job, however. They contain spores. Some mushrooms, like puffballs, burst open to release their spores. Others, such as stinkhorns, produce spores in a stinky slime.

FUNGI Facts

Most fungi don't produce mushrooms. They release their spores in other ways. Some, like molds, develop spores on their hyphae!

A puffball mushroom releases its spores. It belongs to a group of puffballs called *Lycoperdon*, which means "wolf fart"!

THE GREAT RECYCLERS

One of fungi's key roles is as **decomposers**. Imagine what the world would look—and smell—like without decomposers. Living things die every day. In fact, there are billions of tons of dead things that pile up each year. Thanks in part to fungi, the world is not covered in the remains of dead stuff. One group of fungi eats dead plants and animals. Magpie mushrooms, for example, eat dead grasses. Lion's mane and oyster mushrooms eat dead wood.

Lion's mane mushroom

Seashell-shaped oyster mushrooms grow in clusters. They can be found on dead or living trees. Over time, the enzymes this fungus produces break down the wood. The result is white rot. Wood is made of two main substances—cellulose and lignin. Cellulose is the chief part of plant cell walls. Lignin acts as a glue that binds cellulose together. White rot targets lignin, causing the wood to get soft and lose strength. Wood affected by white rot appears white and stringy.

Oyster mushrooms

FUNGI Facts

Oyster mushrooms are also carnivorous. They trap, kill, and eat little wormlike animals called nematodes!

Other fungi cause brown rot. This type of rot mostly attacks cellulose. The result is reddish-brown wood that shatters into cube-like pieces. Wood-decaying fungi return nutrients, such as nitrogen and phosphorus, to the soil. They also help create and enrich the soil. “Without the fungi, we wouldn’t have soil,” said John Michelotti, a mycologist. All of these things benefit plant growth.

Another fungus tackles one of nature's toughest materials—animal horns. The horn stalkball grows on keratin, the stuff that makes up hair, fingernails, and horns. Eventually, it gobbles up all the keratin. A similar fungus can be found on owl pellets. These are the "leftovers" that owls cough up after a meal. Owl pellets are about as big as an adult's thumb. They're usually made up of small bones, fur, and feathers. The fungus efficiently breaks down everything but the bones!

A purple jellydisc fungus

FUNGI Facts

Purple jellydisc is another fungus that decomposes dead wood. This odd-looking mushroom looks like brains.

The hat thrower fungus has a favorite food as well. Cow poop! Spreading its spores isn't easy, though. Grazing cows avoid eating grass near their poop. So, the fungus has evolved a trick. Using a tiny fluid-filled bladder, it can shoot its spores up to 6 feet (1.8 meters). When the bladder expands, pressure causes it to push the fluid and the spores into the air. They land far away from the poop pile on a fresh patch of grass. Then the cows eat the spores and poop them out. Another hot meal for the hat thrower fungus—and less poop!

These are hat thrower fungus bladders and spores. After cows eat the spores, they pass through the animals' digestive systems.

One company, Hiro Technologies, is harnessing the power of fungi to deal with poop, namely dirty diapers. A baby uses about 3,000 diapers a year. The diapers contain plastic. Plastic can take 500 years to decompose in a landfill. In recent years, scientists have discovered fungi that eat plastic! So, the company developed a packet filled with fungi. Once placed on a dirty diaper, it starts growing. After a couple weeks, the fungi start decomposing the plastic diaper. "It's safe, easy, and you can see with your own naked eyes how plastic gets broken down," said Tero Isokauppila, who works for the company.

In the United States, around 27 billion diapers are tossed into landfills each year.

FUNGI Facts

A fungus called *Pestalotiopsis microspora* is known to break down certain types of plastic.

Experts are also exploring ways in which fungi might help address global plastic waste. Humans produce around 400 million tons of plastic garbage each year. That's equal to the weight of all the people on the planet! Only about 10 percent of plastic gets recycled. In 2017, scientists found a fungus that breaks down plastic in a landfill in Pakistan. Today, hundreds of known species of fungi can aid in decomposing plastic.

A fungal species that lives in the ocean could assist with our plastic problem. The fungus was found in the Great Pacific Garbage Patch. The "garbage patch" is a vast area of floating trash. It's the largest collection of ocean plastic in the world. With the help of sunlight, the fungus may be able to **degrade** plastic. Scientists are excited about using it and other fungi to possibly help deal with plastic pollution.

FUNGI Facts

Using fungi to break down pollution is called mycoremediation (MAHY-koh-rih-mee-dee-AY-shuhn). However, this is a new field that requires more research.

Mountains of plastic trash at a landfill

Breaking it Down

Fungi may also help address other forms of pollution. For decades, companies have been **extracting** oil from the Amazon rainforest. Huge pipelines transport the **fossil fuel**. Sometimes, these pipelines break, resulting in oil spills. Oil is toxic and can kill animals, plants, and people. It also pollutes the land and water. The effects can last for decades. Giant fungi, however, may be able to act as a cleanup crew. They grow in the oil spills and could break down the harmful liquid. The fungi may also absorb **heavy metals**, such as mercury.

Additionally, some fungi might help store carbon. Carbon is a dangerous **greenhouse gas**. And it's a leading cause of **climate change**. Plants supply fungi that live in soil with carbon-rich food. The fungi may be able to store large amounts of that carbon. However, scientists are still working to better understand the relationship between fungi and carbon.

FUNGI Facts

The Amazon rainforest has been called the "lungs of the planet." Why? The forest draws in carbon dioxide and creates the oxygen needed by humans to breathe.

Other fungi may feast on nuclear radiation! When nuclear power plants fail, they can release radiation into the environment. This form of energy damages cells and **DNA**. It can cause cancer or even death. In addition to hurting living things, radiation can pollute the soil and water for many years. Interestingly, there are dark-colored fungi that appear to thrive in radiation. The fungi contain melanin (MEL-uh-nin), the same substance that gives color to our skin and eyes. Some experts think these fungi could use radiation to grow. This process is not well understood. But experts are learning more every day.

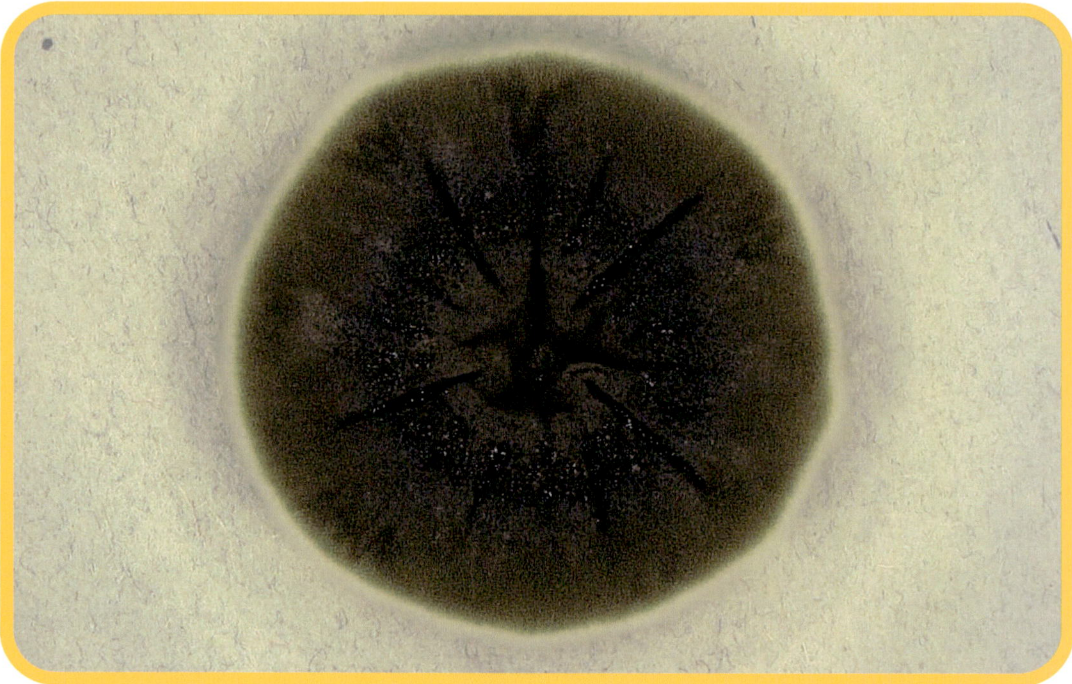

The melanin in the black fungus may help protect it from radiation.

In the future, fungi might even be helpful in space, where there are high levels of radiation. To test this idea, scientists sent the special black fungi to the International Space Station. They studied their growth. Scientists are curious to know whether the fungi could be used to shield astronauts from harmful radiation. Also, understanding how radiation affects fungi could help experts to protect people better on Earth.

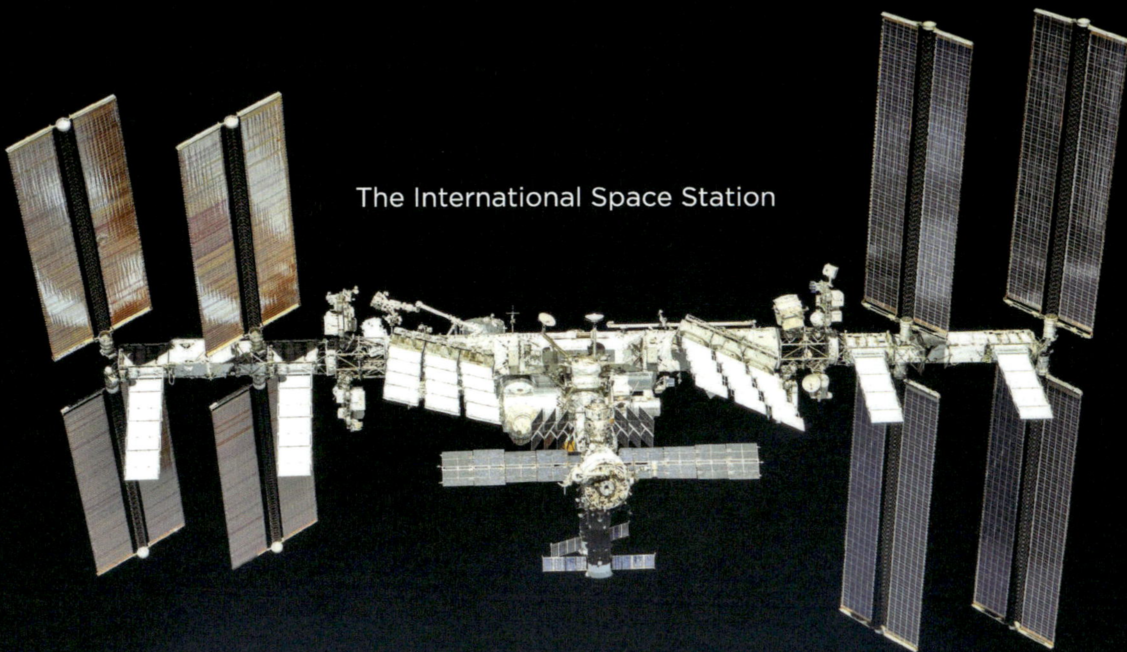

The International Space Station

FUNGI Facts

The International Space Station is a large spacecraft that orbits Earth. It serves as a giant science lab and is home to astronauts from around the world.

Looking Ahead

Our fungi friends remind us that even the smallest things can make a huge difference. Fungi are the world's most powerful recyclers. They can break down harmful human-made substances. They also work to transform dead things into soil and nutrients that plants and other creatures need to thrive. "It's how everything is reborn," says scientist Rob Dunn. "So that this entire web of life is connected, and it's connected through the fungi."

So, the next time you see a mushroom, remember how hard it's working. "The best thing you can do with fungi is accept it, enjoy it, and appreciate what it's doing," said John Michelotti.

FUNGI Facts

Mushrooms can be poisonous. So, if you're not sure a mushroom is safe, don't touch or eat it!

WHO KNEW?
FUN-gi Facts

Hair Ice Fungus

Why does that log have a wispy, white beard? Hair ice, also known as frost beard, is a combination of a fungus and ice. The fungus, *Exidiopsis effusa*, grows on dead wood. It pulls water from the wood. When the air is cold enough, the water freezes. The curious result is ice strands that look like a white beard! Each strand is about the width of a human hair and can grow up to 8 inches (20 cm) long. Sometimes, the ice strands curl, giving them the look of icy wool.

Mushroom House Guests

You may think you're living alone. But you probably have more house guests than you ever imagined. The average home contains 600 to 2,000 species of fungi! Fungal spores enter homes through doors and windows, on food, and even on Christmas trees. Some grow on dust, fabrics, floors, and walls, especially in homes that are warm and moist. Most of the time, these fungi are not dangerous. However, if you have asthma or allergies, these uninvited guests can worsen these health problems.

Goodbye, Dinosaurs

Some experts believe that fungal diseases may have contributed to the extinction of the dinosaurs. After a giant asteroid hit Earth over 66 million years ago, the planet cooled. Cold-blooded dinosaurs were unable to increase their body temperature. And they became more likely to get fungal diseases. Warm-blooded mammals, however, could fight these diseases. This idea could help explain what happened to our dinosaur pals.

GLOSSARY

carbon dioxide (KAR-buhn dye-AHK-side) a colorless, odorless gas that is released when gas, oil, and other fossil fuels are burned; it is also produced by plants

cells (SELZ) the smallest parts of a living thing

climate change (KLYE-mit CHAYNJ) the warming of Earth's air and oceans due to environmental changes, such as a buildup of greenhouse gases

decomposers (dee-kuhm-POHZ-uhrz) living things that rot or break down other things

degrade (dih-GRAYD) to break down

DNA (DEE-EN-AY) short for deoxyribonucleic acid; the molecule that carries the genetic code for a living thing

enzymes (EN-zahymz) substances that cause chemical reactions, such as digestion

evolved (ih-VOLVD) changed over time

extracting (ek-STRAKT-ing) removing something

fossil fuel (FAHS-uhl FYOOL) a fuel such as coal, oil, and gas that's made from the remains of plants and animals that died millions of years ago

germinates (JUR-muh-nayts) begins to grow or develop

greenhouse gas (GREEN-hows GAS) carbon dioxide, methane, and other gases that trap warm air in the atmosphere

heavy metals (HEV-ee MET-uhlz) metals that are often toxic to humans and other living things

mycologist (mahy-KAHL-uh-jist) a person who studies fungi

nutrients (NOO-tree-uhnts) substances needed by fungi and other living things to grow and be healthy

organic (or-GAN-ik) describes a material that was once living, such as dead leaves

organism (OR-guh-niz-uhm) a living thing

photosynthesis (foh-tuh-SIN-thuh-siss) the way plants make food using water, carbon dioxide, and sunlight

pungent (PUHN-juhnt) having a sharp smell or taste

reproduction (ree-pruh-DUHK-shuhn) the creation of offspring

species (SPEE-sheez) certain types of animals or plants that have shared characteristics

LEARN MORE

BOOKS

Boddy, Lynne. *Humongous Fungus*. New York: DK, 2021.

Bonkoski, Ariel. *Mushrooms & Fungi for Kids*. New York: Adventure Publications, 2025.

Gravel, Elise. *The Mushroom Fan Club*. Montreal, Canada: Drawn and Quarterly, 2018.

Plants & Fungi. New York: DK, 2023.

WEBSITES

Explore these online sources with an adult:

Fungi Foundation: Fungi Education
Kids Britannica: Fungus
Maine Audubon: Fungi, the Original Recyclers
New York Botanical Garden: Fungi and Lichens
PBS Learning Media: Fungi

INDEX

ABOUT THE AUTHOR

Joyce Markovics has written hundreds of books for kids. She lives in an old house along the Hudson River. Joyce is fascinated by fungi and what we don't yet know about these extraordinary life-forms. She would like to dedicate this book to Nicole, an extraordinary human and friend whose partnerships rival those of fungi and plants, and express gratitude to mycologist David Hibbett for his expertise and generosity in creating this book.